GET INTERVIEW

JULIE HOLMWOOD

DEDICATION

I have met so many amazing, skilled, talented people who struggle to get interviews for jobs they are absolutely perfect for. When I've taken the time to talk to someone and really get to know their background I can clearly see their strengths. Unfortunately, the modern interview process doesn't work on a get to know you from the get-go basis. First you have to pass the paper exercise of getting someone's attention via your CV and covering letter. Tricky for some, impossible for others, mostly it isn't lack of talent and ability to do the job that makes hiring managers pass you by. It is the lack of relevant information, well presented, within your CV.

You have been my motivation for writing this book. My desire to help you put your best foot forward and show those employers exactly how great you are.

Working hard, becoming skilled and having a strong work ethic is your job.

Helping you convey that in four pages or less within a CV is mine.

Together we can get you that interview!

CONTENTS

ACKNOWLEDGMENTS

I would like to thank my former bosses at the Herald and Post, who channeled my work energy into their recruitment section, long before I realised that recruitment was a job option.

That led me into my first job as a recruiter. Almost twelve years later, I decided to help the people that fell through my gaps and work with more job seekers in a way that would best help them achieve their aims; namely to get that job.

Thank you to all of my recruitment clients, (employers and candidates), who gave me the time and space to ever improve my recruitment knowledge and skills.

Thank you to everyone who has been a part of Churchill Brook. It has been a great journey and we are still only at the very beginning! Exciting times ahead…

Last, but by no means least, thank YOU for letting me help you get that interview. This is just the tip of the iceberg of our offerings to get you that job. Please do reach out if we can help you with any other parts of your job search.

PROLOGUE

Are you frustrated with sending your CV out and never hearing back from anyone? Are you really good at what you do, but just can't get any interviews? Is it difficult to know what else you can do? Do you just wish you could get in front of someone so they could see how great you are for the job?

You're not alone and there is nothing wrong with you. It just takes a different type of CV to grab their attention. Here, for the first time, I reveal all of my secrets and share with you how I have done it successfully, for people like you, thousands of times before.

When your CV speaks for itself the interviews will start, allowing you to do the rest.

1 – MAKING AN APPLICATION

You've found a vacancy that you want to apply for. That's great. You're another step nearer to your dream job now. Time to make the all-important application!

'The closest to perfection a person ever comes is when he fills out a job application form'

Stanley J Randall

However you found out about the role will normally tell you how to apply too. Companies might ask for you to send your CV via email or post it online through their website.

Agencies the same. A headhunter might want to work with you to write your CV so that it is tailored to the role and company. Your friend might want to take it into their boss. Whichever way you are going to do this, one thing remains the same.

This is your only chance to make a first impression

Your objective at this stage is to get an interview. So how are you going to do that?

Start by spending time on the company's website. Get a feeling for what they are like as an organisation. If there are sections about their employees or their hiring process, read them. Then review what you know about the role. What have you got to offer and why will they want to hire you over any other candidate? These are crucial things to include in your application.

Write notes on things you want to let the Company know, which you believe will inspire them to interview you.

This is important groundwork. Before you start to think about writing your CV or covering letter do your research. You need to understand who the Company are and exactly what they are going to want from you.

EXERCISES

- Create an action-step plan that you will now follow for *every* job application. This should include time on the Company's website and thoroughly reading the job description. It might also include looking up the Company on Google or checking for connections on LinkedIn.

- Write a list of the key things people are impressed by, when you're talking about work. What is it that you say about what you do that gets the most positive attention?

- Think about your current or most recent boss. What is it that you do that makes you valuable to them? What would they say makes you good at what you do?

Notes

....

....

....

....

....

....

....

NOTES

....

....

....

....

....

....

....

....

....

....

....

....

....

....

....

....

2 – THE COVERING LETTER

One of the things you need to prepare is a good covering letter (or email). This is your big chance to make a first impression so take your time. Get your coach to read it when you've finished and read it again yourself the day after writing it, to make sure you are still pleased with it before sending it to the Company.

Start with Dear *whoever*. Make sure you spell the person's name correctly!

In your first paragraph state what you are applying for and where you heard about the opportunity. This informs the recipient which position your application refers to.

The second paragraph should be all about you in relation to this particular role. For example if the role calls for three years+ experience coaching children between the ages of five and eight, with knowledge of business and marketing, you might write the following:

I have fifteen years experience working with children, predominantly as a teacher for 5 – 8 year olds. During that time I have frequently been commended by my colleagues, superiors and parents for my ability to encourage the best effort and behaviour from my charges. I have recently undertaken a distance learning course with the Open University to complete my MBA. My dissertation was a business plan with specific focus on how strong marketing creates desire within the market and improves sales. Having studied this opportunity and researched your Company I think there is a lot I could bring to this role and I would be delighted to come and discuss this with you in more detail.

The final paragraph wraps up your application and goes something like this: I have enclosed a copy of my CV for your perusal. I look forward to hearing your thoughts.

Then finish with yours sincerely if it is a letter, or kind regards for an email, your full name and telephone number(s).

Make sure you attach your (tailored) CV!

Finally SPELL CHECK, SPELL CHECK, SPELL CHECK.

I have watched hiring managers delete CVs purely on misspelled words. The up and downside of computers: the upside is that it is easy for you to check your spelling; the downside is any errors will highlight themselves in red type the moment the hiring manager looks at your CV. Remember how bad school work looked when it was covered with the teachers red pen? Imagine sending that piece of highlighted work as part of your job application… you do, when your spelling isn't perfect.

EXERCISES

- Write a list of the key achievements, experience and skills you have that are asked for in the job description. You should be able to see at least five.

- Create the body paragraphs for your covering letter with these points.

- From your Company research, list a key point that makes you want to work for this organisation. Include it near the top of your letter. Possibly as part of paragraph one. Think about how great it is to receive a personal letter or email; this is the same with job applications. Companies love to receive a well-thought out, personal letter that answers two of their three key questions:

  - Can you do the job?
  - Will you love the job?
  - …The third question will be answered at interview; can they tolerate working with you?

Notes

....

....

....

....

NOTES

....

....

....

....

....

....

....

....

....

....

....

....

....

....

....

3 – WHAT IS A CV?

A CV (curriculum vitae), or resume in some parts of the world, is a short factual document about you, your work history, skills and experience.

When well written, it tells the hiring Company exactly why you will be good (or even great) at doing the job they are currently recruiting for.

A good CV is essential when you are looking for a new role. I cannot stress how important it is to take your time to get it right. This is your personal equivalent of a marketing brochure. It is going to sell who you are and what you can do to a potential employer, enough to get them to want to know more and therefore call you forward for interview.

Basic tips include:

- The layout should be neat and tidy and easy for someone to read.

- Should be kept to a maximum of four sides of A4 (unless otherwise stated by the Company).

- Be positive about all of the relevant things you have done in relation to the type of role you are applying for.

- Be accurate. A lot of companies will double check your information on any social media profiles you have. Most companies will then take references. Many go one step further and include background screening in their recruitment process. This means that all dates, job titles, qualifications and specific achievements will be verified. Most employers don't mind what grade you got in your exams; they do care that you're honest!

- Be spelled correctly; use your spell checker!

EXERCISES

- Double check all of your education qualifications (and grades if you're going to list them within your CV). This is the key area that people get wrong on their CV. *If you know you got an A Level in Geography but can't remember, or find, which grade, just include 'A Level Geography'.*

- Double check all of your employment dates. You can list jobs in terms of years, ie 2004 – 2008, or you can add months if you know them, for example June 2006 – December 2009.

- Double check other facts and figures you want to include within your CV. Only include specific data if you know that it is accurate. *It is better to be more general and truthful, than specific and give false information. If discovered, this will not only lose you the job opportunity, it will also call into question your integrity.*

Notes

....

....

....

....

....

NOTES

....

....

....

....

....

....

....

....

....

....

....

....

....

....

....

4 – CV CATEGORIES

Some time ago Fortune Magazine printed some quotes from real life CV's, including

and

. Both great sentiments and definitely attention grabbing, but not necessarily going to get you the right response from every potential employer.

So, what should you put into your CV and what should you leave out? Let's start with the headings:

Professional Profile – this is a summary of who you are and what you do. It should always be tailored to the job you are applying for and should give the hiring manager a snapshot of what you can do for their Company.

Professional Experience – this is your career history. Start with what you are doing now and work your way backwards. Remember dates and job titles will typically be verified if you are offered the job, so keep them accurate! Again, this should be tailored to the job you're applying for. If there are ten things you could say about your current job, but you've decided to only say five, pick the five which are relevant to the vacancy you're responding to.

Professional Training – every course, certification, accreditation and training you have had that's relevant to this type of role and anything notable that isn't

Education – whatever you left formal education with, even if it is just two GCSEs. If you left school more than ten years ago then the grades and subjects are mostly irrelevant, except where the Company has stated otherwise

Additional Information – optional subject to add all those other bits that you want the Company to know about you because they are relevant and show you in the light you wish to be seen in

Personal Details – you no longer need to state your age, date of birth or nationality but you should disclose your location, and you may want to include your marital status and information about your driving licence if the role is going to involve travel

Hobbies and Interests – this section shows the employer more about you the person and helps them to round out what you might be like

References – it's not essential to name anyone on your CV but I would state that references will be made available on request

A good CV will open every door for you. Give these subject headers some thought while we look at what to include within each section.

EXERCISES

- Great CVs are *always* tailored to the role you're applying for. Give some thought to the general information you want to include. Write a list of the subject headers you are going to use in your CV and if you're a lover of doing all things electronically, create and save the list as your CV template.

- Place all of the checked dates and job titles of your career history into your template (leave the descriptions until you have a vacancy in mind). In most cases you should go back about twenty years *or* to your first job if you either haven't had many jobs or you're very young.

- Include all of your education, personal details and hobbies and interests.

- Add any generic and notable professional training courses.

- Create a header and footer within your document. In the header place your address and contact details. Don't forget to include your email address, even if you always submit your CV electronically. The hiring manager may print this out and you want contacting you to be easy. In the footer place your name and the month and year you are submitting this CV. Again the name helps someone keep your CV together if they print it. The date helps if you're kept on file for a couple of months.

This will form your basic CV template that you can now tailor to each job you want to apply for.

NOTES

....

....

....

....

....

....

....

....

....

....

....

....

....

....

....

5 - CV CONTENT

This is the perfect vacancy. You always wanted to move from marketing into business development. You know that you can do it. You know you have all the relevant experience; you've been doing the job for the past six months since the restructure.

This role is perfect. Hand on heart you can honestly say 'yes, I have that' to every single requirement on the job description. So, why, when you write your CV does it say everything about your marketing experience and nothing about business development? Is it because the hiring manager is a mind reader? Or because you are waiting to wow them with the big surprise that you are indeed perfect for the role when you meet at the interview? I would suggest neither is actually true, because your CV just fell foul to the delete key.

So what *should* you say?

The total of your combined work experience does not fit into four (or less) pages of A4. It is therefore not only reasonable, but expected, that you only give an overview of what you have done and not list every single task, action and achievement you have ever had.

Rather than add a new paragraph to a static document every time you revamp your CV, my suggestion is rewrite it. Using the template you created from the last chapter, start from the end and work back.

In this case the new job is your starting point; *I want a role in business development*. Now work back from there.

What have you been doing in your current role that is relevant to business development? Wow, you have been doing the role for six months, how fantastic, you have the right experience. Now, your last role, what was relevant to a role in business development there? You were dealing with customers, before they ordered. Great! Plus you worked on identifying new markets, fantastic. The role before … you get the picture?

Your CV should be honest and factual; that's a given. It should also be relevant. You are creating a document that markets the skills and experience you have gained to-date that are relevant to the role you are applying for. Of course you can list some things that aren't, but keep them in perspective.

If the role is for finance director and you have been doing the tasks as part of your current job as operations manager you can say; duties commensurate with running a £10m operation across Europe. But if the role you're applying for doesn't need someone with skills in logistics management, don't waste five bullet points detailing everything you have done in that area. Instead, use the space to talk about everything you have done that is listed in the vacancy job description.

Did I already mention keeping it relevant?

EXERCISES

- Thinking about the jobs you want to apply for, write a list of the key skills (minimum of five) that make you right for this kind of role.

- What other skills and experience do you have that is relevant? Write down all of the things that immediately spring to mind and come back and add to it every time you remember something else

Silly story: *During a radio interview I was asked about remarkable things I had done that had shifted my perception of what I was capable of and enabled me to think outside of my own limiting box. I really struggled to find an answer and ended up mumbling something that was uninteresting, uninspiring and insignificant. I completely forgot that when I was 25 I'd done a firewalk! Twice I had taken seven steps across burning coals. Afterwards I was invincible! I mean, if you can walk on fire you can do anything, right? Exactly! It was the perfect answer to the interviewer's question and yet, put on the spot, I completely forgot about it!*

Doing these exercises in advance will give you the buffer of time, to remember all of those amazing things that have fallen to the back of your memory. Maybe your new job calls for Spanish and you did a gap year in Madrid?

NOTES

....

....

....

....

....

....

....

....

....

....

....

....

....

....

....

....

6 - THE CV THAT GETS INTERVIEWS

When it comes to making job applications, go for quality not quantity. Sending out your CV fifty times in one day is not going to make you more likely to get a job. In fact the opposite might be true, as your applications will be un-thought out and not clearly targeted.

Pick the companies you apply to carefully and know that you are a great fit for both them as an organisation and the role. If you fall in love with a company and haven't seen the right opening, send in a speculative application indicating what you can do and the strengths you can bring to them because... (fill in the blanks). Remember to clearly mark your application as speculative and find the most appropriate person to send it to. Most likely, it will be someone within the Human Resources department

Tailor your CV to *each* and *every* application. I know it takes time, it's a fiddle and sometimes it will have you sat scratching your head. But if you want the interview, you need to look like a fit for the role.

I was constantly amazed by the great emails I received from people who were the perfect match to the role I was working on. Their covering letters were exactly what I was searching for. Then I would open the CV and it wouldn't match. There would be nothing in it that was relevant; delete.

During your career you have done enough tasks to fill a book and now you are trying to pick the edited highlights for a two to four page CV. It sounds easy, but knowing what to select and even worse, what to leave out, is actually harder than including everything and turning it into a book.

How do you pick the right things to include?

You read the job spec for the role you are applying for. You go through *every* item listed in the company's requirements. Create a bullet point within your CV and detail your experience in that area.

Cover each point that you can. Don't make things up. If there are two points that you don't have at all, then you will just have to miss them off. But for everything you do have, clearly list it.

Do this for every role. So if you have had four previous jobs and you have been doing something relevant to the role that you are applying for in the last three, create the bullet points for each of those three.

Often the other role(s) will have some transferable skills so, you will need to get creative, but with some thought you will be able to come up with an interesting profile there too.

The example I have created is for a Marketing Manager

Company Requirements	Your Experience
Five years product marketing experience	Seven years product marketing experience
Running advertising campaigns	Managed advertising campaigns for six products using online and paper based media
Brand development	Led the brand development of three new products which were brought to market to fill a gap within the B2C sector
Monitoring web traffic	Took responsibility for managing Google analytics and targeting our online efforts accordingly
Social media management	Created and implemented our social media strategy, driving 10,000 additional unique visitors to our website per month for six months to date and increasing sales by £500K over the same period

Customer satisfaction management	Increased the profile of our organisation using customer retention strategies and social media, to be more customer friendly and improve our engagement strategy
Manage a team of three marketing assistants	Managed two direct reports and had a dotted line report for our Internal Sales Executive

When the job spec from the company looks like the left hand column and the CV you submit looks like the right hand column, you look a great match.

When I'm in charge of candidate selection, this person is definitely on the interview list.

You might have done many other things that you are more proud of, or would typically list, but this is not about what you think about you. This is about what they will think about you.

This is not about what you think about you. This is about what they will think about you.

If the company wants what is on the left and you submit a list that doesn't reflect that in any way, shape, or form, the fact that you have done all of the things in the right hand column will not be clear. The hiring manager will not be able to read between lines that you don't write and they won't be psychic enough to work it out.

MAKE IT OBVIOUS!

If in doubt, spell it out so they can see your points.

If you look at a job spec and you only have two skills out of the ten requirements listed by the company, you are <u>not</u> a match and making an application is probably going to be a waste of time. I would recommend that you have more than half of what the Company are looking for.

If there are ten requirements, I would suggest you need six or above, for the role to be a possible fit for you. Remember, there is no shortage of vacancies and there are more than enough companies currently hiring. You don't need to try and fit your round-peg-self into a square hole. Your time and energy will be much better spent looking for a round hole.

This will up your chances of being hired and will increase your job satisfaction after you're in post.

Key point: if you get the job, you might be in that company, doing that role forty hours a week, for the next three years (or more). That's over 5000 hours of your life that you'll never get back! Is getting this job going to be a good thing? Will it be what you want? Do you really want to make this application?

If the answer is 'yes' and you do really want this job, then the time and effort required to make this a good application is going to be time well spent.

Remember, it is your job to make your application attractive to the company you are applying to. Take as much time as you need to do this, do it well and you will only be doing it a few times before you get that new job!

EXERCISES

- Using the vacancy you are want to apply for, create a tailored CV using the list of skills in the vacancy advert or job specification to write your job history details into your CV template. Consider the skills you need to demonstrate when writing each job description, from your current or last job, back.

- Using the same vacancy, add all of the relevant courses and training you have taken.

- Now write a good professional profile by summarising all of the relevant areas of your skills and experience into a couple of short paragraphs. Place this at the top of your CV, just under your name, so it gets read first.

- Is there any additional information you should include (like that gap year in Madrid or firewalking) that will enhance this application?

- Do this as a separate exercise for all of the open vacancies you want to submit applications for.

Notes

....

....

....

NOTES

....

....

....

....

....

....

....

....

....

....

....

....

....

....

....

7 - WHEN YOU NEED A JOB

Sometimes, you're in a spot and you just want any job so that you can pay your bills and breathe more easily. You might be more concerned with the next three months than long-term career satisfaction. I understand that kind of motivator. Try to become even more focused on tailoring your CV for each role and making sure that you are a great fit. This will work to get you that interview.

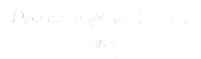

Focus on finding a way to relax your worry and tension. See if you can find some ways to take the pressure off yourself a little. Work out how long you can really afford to survive financially and try to come up with a solution in case you don't find a job right away.

Do you have something you can sell? Do you have access to borrowing money? Can you rent out a room in your house? Are there any odd jobs that you can do locally that will give you some 'tide-over' cash? Try to take the pressure off yourself, because desperate people don't interview well; that is the real truth behind the cliché, that it is easier to get a job when you already have one.

Employers typically don't have a preference for hiring people who are working over those who are not. More, the person that is employed has an air of confidence and assuredness that puts the interviewer at ease. There is an unwritten process that says 'I can trust you, because you trust yourself'

EXERCISES

- Taking all the luxuries out of your budget in the short-term, how many weeks or months can you afford to be job-hunting? Sit down and do a proper analysis of your finances and decide just how urgent your job search is.

- Work out what else you can do to buy some time. Is there anything you can sell? Do you have any talents you can offer locally to generate some immediate income?

- Make a list of any agencies that supply temporary workers in your field. Contact each one and register your details. Remember, this is not a career step. This is purely to take the financial pressure off, giving you the freedom of time to find the right role

If you already have enough money for the next three months and you find a way to generate half your desired salary, you now have enough money for the next six months.

Notes

....

....

....

....

....

NOTES

8 - GENERALLY THIS CV WORKS

Sometimes you need a general CV. It gives you something to send to recruitment agencies and enables you to make speculative applications to companies. But you still need to do it in a targeted way so that it works in your favour, because you still want it to get you a positive response and to generate interviews. For that to happen it needs to be anything but general.

Here's how: Set aside a few hours for this. Bear in mind what you want to achieve; a new role. Think about the salary that it will command. You are more than justified to spend half a day on this project. Longer if you need to.

Let's say that you have narrowed your job search down to two options. Maybe you have been working as a dental receptionist and now you want to either work in a dental environment or you would be happy to be a receptionist somewhere else. That is two different CV's; not one that is an either or story. Even when your CV is general it needs to be focused.

Decide on an exact role (if you have more than one repeat this exercise for each). Now go and find four job specs for this position. Google is good for this, or you might be lucky enough to have some job specs in your inbox from positions you've already spotted.

Printing them out so that you can put them side by side is a good idea. Or just flick from screen to screen, whichever you're most comfortable with.

Identify which requirements are in all four specs. These are now at the top of your list to address in your (anything but) general CV. Create a bullet point for each one and list your achievements within that area.

For example, if you are a Business Continuity Manager;

Company Requirements	Your Experience
Three years relevant experience	Five years experience as a Business Continuity Manager, predominantly within the telecommunications industry
Incident management	Managed twelve major incidents, including a move to our back-up site following a flood. Also involved with three third-party supplier incidents
BS25999	Used BS25999 to ensure a recognised standard was adhered to and that we could align with our supply chain

Writing policies	Wrote the business continuity plan for our end-user division which consisted of twenty-five documents, all of which were adopted at board level
Conducting tests	Wrote a format for twice yearly testing which we then ran across the organisation. I was responsible for coordinating the involvement and creating post test reports

Now see which requirements are on three of the specs and create the bullet points as above. Then two and if you still don't have much down, look at the individual requirements that are unique to each job spec. You want to create a minimum of eight bullets and a maximum of twelve for this to be a good, strong, informative CV that gives lots of information without becoming the sequel to War and Peace.

Next go to your previous job and do the same. You should detail your last three jobs, giving five to eight bullets on number two and three. Unless the fourth job you list happened within the last ten years you can write a minimal amount. It is perfectly acceptable to just list the company name, dates and your job title for things that happened a long time ago.

This is the most perfect general CV you can create. You are addressing mainstream requirements for the role you are interested in and most companies looking to fill that position will find your profile of interest.

This works best when your last few years of experience are in the industry you wish to be in for the foreseeable future.

Take time doing this, work on it, spell check it, perfect it, go to bed and look at it again the following day.

Use this to apply for roles that hold the job title you searched against, when you don't have enough information to create a fully targeted CV.

EXERCISES

- Decide the exact job you are now looking for. Find and print off four job specs for this type of role. They don't have to be current, or roles that you will definitely apply for and you don't need to know who the companies are. They are purely for research purposes; to help you create a general CV.

- Going through the specs side-by-side identify the skills and experience that all four are looking for. Once you have a list of all of the points within all four specs, count them up. Do you have eight or more? If you do, stop. If you don't, identify the requirements that appear in three... then two ... if you still have less than eight start listing the requirements that are unique to each post.

- Starting with your current or last role, create a bullet point in response to the top requirement on your newly created list. (See the examples on pages 26 and 37). Now a bullet that relates to the second point... and so on until you have between eight and twelve bullets – make sure they all contain the information and any specific achievements that relate to it. *Achievements are the icing on the CV cake and are what sets you apart from the other applicants.*

- Continue your career history by matching five to eight achievements of your three previous roles against your list.

- At the top of each job history write a two to three line overview of what your job entailed. This should tie

Exercises continued...

together your bullet points and summarise what your job is (or was) about, without being repetitive.

- Looking at all of the skills required in each of the roles, add all of the relevant courses and training you have taken.

- Now write a couple of short paragraphs for your professional profile, by summarising what you've written about your career skills and experience. Place this at the top of your CV, just under your name, so it gets read first.

- Is there any additional information you should include (like that gap year in Madrid or firewalking) that will enhance this application?

Because this CV is now a pretty good match to four separate vacancies within your chosen field there is a great chance that it will interest recruiters for vacancies they have. You are certainly giving yourself the best chance with this tailored general CV.

Notes

....

....

....

NOTES

....

....

....

....

....

....

....

....

....

....

....

....

....

....

....

9 – LISTING ACHIEVEMENTS WITHIN YOUR CV

'Winners compare their
achievements with their goals, while
losers compare their achievements
with those of other people'

Nido Qubein

In CV terms, listing your achievements shows a potential employer what you actually accomplish when you get to work. You know that a job has a list of duties, all jobs do. And you know that to do that job you have to perform the list of duties on a regular, if not daily, basis. So what sets you aside from the rest?

The one thing that is going to make you stand out from the crowd of applicants that have a somewhat similar list of past job titles to you is your achievements! Pure and simple. What you actually accomplished when you got to work. This is the part of your CV that spells H-O-P-E to your prospective boss. The thing that makes him/her think you will be the right person to hire and an asset to the team.

> *The one thing that makes you stand out from the crowd of applicants is your achievements*

What should you list and where should you put them within your now fabulous CV.

A job spec is a list of tasks contained within a role. A list of achievements is what you have done in relation to that list. Make sure you list the latter.

If you are applying for the role of Accounts Assistant then some things are obvious; of course you use spreadsheets, software and are good with numbers.

What is it that makes you great at what you do?

- What have you done?
- Where have you been commended?
- What have you achieved?
- What do people compliment you on?

These are the things that are going to set you apart from every other candidate, so list them.

Start at the end. Go back to the job specification of the role you are applying for and see if they are looking for you to be able to achieve anything within their organisation. If so and if you already have achievements in those areas there is your starting point.

On top of that list anything and everything you got commended, awarded and generally praised for in your previous roles. You should be able to list at least two achievements per role for your last ten years of employment (which is probably two or three jobs). Ideally you will be able to think of five.

List them under the section that talks about your responsibilities so that the document flows. For example;

Sales Manager
Running the European team I had responsibility for five Sales Executives (external) and two Account Managers (internal). I also managed ten key accounts within the financial sector, typically working on deals in excess of £1.5m … (so on and so forth)

Achievements;
- Grew the revenue in my region by 300% in two years, from £5m to £15m
- Grew my team from three external and one internal to the current five external and two internal as a result of the increased revenue generation
- Won a long weekend to a five star health spa for being Sales Person of the quarter, Q3 2011
- Received a personal email from the Chairman commending me on my contribution to the Company's overall success as a direct result of winning the largest order the Company has won to date

- Voted best team leader in a fun competition run by the European offices in 2010

Don't be shy about this. Blow your own trumpet. You are the only person championing your application at this point, so you have to be your own best friend and really give yourself a big cheer for all the things you have already done well.

If you feel apprehensive about doing this, imagine you are talking about a person you hold in high esteem; your spouse, your child, your best friend. What would you say about their achievements? How much pride and excitement do you feel when you talk about their moments of glory? Use that passion to get your finest times down on paper. It really will make your CV stand out, no matter how many other people have applied for this role!

EXERCISES

- Go back over the CV you've created and make sure all of your achievements are clearly listed.

- Include any achievements related to training courses and education. If you passed a three year course in six months, say so.

- Find all of the emails you've been sent commending your work and print them off. Put together all pictorial or written records of your achievements. Create a folder you can take with you to interview, backing up all of your accomplishments. (Nyrex folders are great for this)

- Double check all of your printouts against your CV. Make sure the data is an exact match.

Notes

....

....

....

....

....

....

NOTES

....

....

....

....

....

....

....

....

....

....

....

....

....

....

....

10 - REFERENCES

A company will typically want to verify some or all of your key information prior to your commencing employment with them. In the majority of cases they will take up references, or invoke background screening, upon your verbal acceptance of the role. Only at this point would I suggest you provide a list of names and contact details for your referees (I would only ever write 'references are available on request' within the CV itself)

Who are you going to pick, what information do you need to provide and what are your referees likely to be asked about you?

In many instances you have to give the name of someone at your last three employers. This doesn't have to be your direct boss. You can name the boss of a team you worked closely with, another member of the senior management team or indeed the HR Director. If you have worked for your current employer a long time and your role is customer facing you can also provide the name of a client.

You should always pick someone that knows, or knew you well, who you worked directly with some of the time and who you got on with professionally. Speak to them first and get their permission. Then provide their name, job title, your relationship to them during the time that you worked together, a daytime telephone number and work email address. Most of the time your referee will be contacted via telephone.

Questions that they may be asked are;

- Can you confirm how long you worked with the candidate and in what relationship?

- Are you able to confirm that the candidate worked for *company* from *date* until *date*?

- In your opinion did the candidate perform their tasks competently and conscientiously?

- How would you rate the candidate's attitude towards work?

- What would you describe as the candidate's key strength and major weakness?

- How would you describe the candidate's relationships with other members of staff, customers and suppliers?

- This is the role we are considering the candidate for; do you think they are a good match?

- Would you re-hire this candidate if the opportunity arose?

- Do you have any additional information you think we should consider with regard to this candidate's application?

This is a small sample of the type of questions people use when taking up references and they give you an idea of the kind of relationship you need to have had with your referee for this line of questioning to be able to highlight you as a positive choice.

When I have been asked to take references on behalf of a client I have spent about twenty minutes on the phone with each referee. A lot of information is exchanged and lots of ground gets covered. Make sure you give careful thought and consideration to whom you choose!

Finally, don't forget to give thanks and gratitude to your referees when the process is complete. Whether they were contacted or not this time, the fact they were willing is enough to warrant a thank you. You never know when you might want to call upon them again.

EXERCISES

- Contact the people you would like to use for references and check that they are happy for you to give their name. Confirm the best telephone number and email address to use

You might be asked for as many as four references. It is worth having that many names to hand.

Notes

....

....

....

....

....

....

....

....

....

....

11 – THE ROLE OF SOCIAL MEDIA

Social Media is now a part of our way of life. Current reports indicate that 80% of companies are using social media for their recruitment and 95% of those 80% use LinkedIn

When I was a headhunter, I used LinkedIn every day. My researcher would run searches against current vacancies we had and see which candidates looked the best fit, as a starting point to our creation of a shortlist. I am not the only one that did this; talking to industry colleagues it seems that is the norm.

What does your LinkedIn profile say about you and what should it say? Even when you need to exercise discretion, because you are linked to your colleagues or even your boss, you can keep a good profile.

The first thing you should consider is that your profile is aimed at selling YOU. That is your purpose if you want a new job. Explaining the ins and outs of the product you are responsible for is fabulous if you want to make product sales, or if you are the product developer, but really you are missing the opportunity to sell yourself.

- Start with your overview; who are you and what do you do that is unique to you? What is it about you and your skills and experience that would make you attractive to a potential employer?

- Professional experience; pasting your job spec gives someone an idea of your tasks but tells them nothing about your ability. What have you done in your role? What were your achievements? What do you contribute to your team / Company? What have you been commended for? What do people consult you about? What are your special skills that only you bring to your current organisation? Everyone knows what an Operations Manager does, what they want to know is how YOU do it and if that makes you a potential match for them.

- Include recommendations; they are easy to request, you can select who you approach and they add an extra layer of verification in your skills and abilities

- Make your profile visible to all. Having a wonderful profile and keeping it secret is as useful to you as having no profile at all. Set your privacy settings so that as many people as possible can see you

- Include ways to contact you. After all, you want to make getting in touch easy

For a FREE guide detailing how to get headhunted via LinkedIn in 10 easy steps please email us at churchillbrook@gmail.com

Companies are also using Social Media sites to run due-diligence checks on applicants. Getting looked up is a good sign, because it means they are interested in hiring you, but you need to check that what they find confirms that decision. Look at the profiles you have on places like Facebook and Twitter

'Don't say anything online that you wouldn't want plastered on a billboard with your face on it.'

Erin Bury

What are you tweeting? Would an employer or potential employer like it?

It is fine to use your social media to focus on your social time. If all your tweets are about fishing and that is your passion, then so be it. But if you are tweeting in general and are overly critical, angry or rude about people or organisations is that giving the right impression? It might read that you are less than easy going and going to be difficult to get along with.

If you're currently employed in a nine-to-five role yet your Facebook page lists streams of Mafia Wars, Farmville or similar posts from weekday daytimes when you should be working, you might want to either change your daily habits, or block the application from posting directly to your news feed.

How about your status updates? Are they upbeat, friendly, chatty and interesting or are they overly critical, angry and/or rude?

What about the groups you are a member of and the pages you like? Are they controversial? If you have an eclectic mix of interests that is good. But if you are supporting pages that are less than kind or publicly unacceptable, then a potential employer might make the wrong assumption about you. Even if they don't have an opinion, they might not want to be associated with something their clients won't like

Have you been posting anywhere about the long lunches, extended shopping trips and exaggerated expense claims you've been getting away with? Are you setting up meetings with friends for social purposes during work hours when you're not on annual leave?

Are you slating your boss or current colleagues?

Is every photo posted from drunken nights out with you semi-conscious or behaving badly?

Any, or a combination of all of these things, seen by somebody that doesn't know you and who has no way of putting this information into the context of you being 'the nicest person Joe Bloggs has ever met' will count against you. That is not to say that you shouldn't have fun, enjoy life or live your life your way, but you should consider how a stranger will perceive you from the limited information they have.

A few drunken pictures are fine, along with a lot of sober ones. The odd 'I'm having a bad day and my boss is not my favourite person' updates are fine, interspersed with anything and everything else.

If in doubt ask your parents or a friend-of-a-friend that doesn't know you to look at your profile and give a synopsis of what they think you are like; you might just get a big surprise!

EXERCISES

- Do you have a profile on LinkedIn? Every job seeker benefits from this site. It is where all of the recruiters and headhunters go to find people. If you don't have a profile, create one.

- Your LinkedIn profile shouldn't be your CV, but use the same techniques to create it. Leave out any achievements or accomplishments your then-employer(s) wouldn't want in the public domain.

- Look at your other social media profiles and check that they are 'job search ready'. Would you be happy for the CEO of the company hiring for your dream job to read your profiles? Would they be happy for their clients to read your profiles? If the answer to either question is no, start making the necessary changes.

- Google your name. See what comes up and double check that is ok for a potential employer to read and/or know about you.

There are lots of reports about people being fired for their social media posts. When you want to be hired you should be even more conservative. If it is down to two applicants and one is being rude and abusive online and the other is not... that is enough to swing the decision. Don't let something really stupid cost you that job!

NOTES

....

....

....

....

....

....

....

....

....

....

....

....

....

....

....

....

ADDITIONAL TIPS AND ADVICE

12 - BANG YOUR OWN DRUM

One of the most common lines I have heard whilst working with jobseekers is: 'I don't like to blow my own trumpet'. My response has always been: 'but who else is going to do it?' I still stand by that as a good answer. However, there is something else

When a company is hiring they are doing so for a business purpose. For example:

'We need to have a Head of Marketing so that our company continues to be promoted, remain in our clients focus and we gain new opportunities to generate revenue.'

This is an easy one to see; we all know that without revenue a company falls into decline. What if you work in the post room? The same thing is true because your role still enables the company to function. The bottom line is this. If your role had no significance then it would not be allocated headcount and salary.

If your role had no significance then it would not be allocated headcount and salary.

I always see an organisation like a car; you might be more familiar with the steering wheel and your seat but without the filters and plugs it wouldn't function. Every part is as necessary as every other to make the whole thing work.

Back to the hiring company... When they are looking for someone to do XYZ of which you are most proficient, but you haven't emphasised that within your CV, you deprive them of the opportunity to add your skills to their organisation and improve their efficiency within the market.

When you are marketing yourself it is not about you singing your praises. It is about you advising someone else as to the full range of your skills and abilities; enabling them to find the help that they most urgently need (you!)

When you put together your covering letter you are not doing it to bang your own drum out of some sense of misplaced ego. You are doing it to let the particular organisation you are applying to, know how you can help them and therefore answer their question. The age old question that we all have. What's in it for me?

When a hiring company review your CV, the question they are asking themselves is:

'What can this person do for us?'

As you start to prepare a new application stick a post-it above your screen, or wherever you are working, with this key line on it 'what's in it for me' and then tailor all of your answers to it. 'Do I have experience in X, Y and Z? Well, this is what I can do for you on that subject …'

EXERCISES

- Run another check on your CV. Have you taken credit for all of the accomplishments and achievements that were yours to claim?

- Have you accurately portrayed your skills and experience so the reader can clearly see exactly how you will benefit their organisation and help them meet a specific business need?

Notes

....

....

....

....

....

....

....

....

....

....

13 – IS ANYBODY OUT THERE?

I recently read that Google receive over one million CVs per year for between 1000-4000 roles. This works out at 250-1000 candidates for every single job. A surprisingly large number? Not really!

When any company advertises their role they can expect up to 1000 applicants in response. I am sure this is part of the reason companies have become focused on only replying to candidates that make the shortlist and ignoring the rest. I know from my time as a frontline recruiter that the percentage of applicants who are inappropriate and/or mismatched, is huge. I regularly received CVs from candidates without a single skill or element of relevant experience. The job-searching spammer or junk mailer.

If you have great skills, are a good match for the roles you are applying for and yet you are receiving no interview requests; obtaining no feedback is frustrating and demoralising. It seems that you send off relevant email after relevant email into a black-hole of nothingness. All the while becoming more anxious that the clock is ticking. So what, other than now hiring me, can you do?

- **Go back to the drawing board.** Do all of the exercises in this book and write a new CV from scratch. When you amend the original it is so tempting to see bullet points you like and although they are not strictly relevant, because you like them, you leave them in. Using either *'The CV That Gets Interviews'* (chapter 6) if you know the exact role in a specific company that you are applying to, or *'Generally This CV Works'* (chapter 8) if you have a job title and want to send it in multiple directions, sit down with a blank sheet of paper and start your CV again. You might be amazed what you write in contrast to the one you have been using.

- **Run a search for agencies that specialise in your specific market.** Find a good consultant that would like to work with you and arrange some time to talk. Telephone is great, or skype, if you are not local enough for a meeting. I rarely met my candidates in the initial stages because of the logistics. Discuss your experience, show them the CV you have prepared and ask for their advice. Get them to suggest ways that you can improve your initial impact, because your CV is going to be one of many that is going to hit the Hiring Manager's desk. A good recruiter will be happy to take the time to help you with your application. They know that helping you get the job with their client equals a happy client and a fee for them.

- **Spend some time identifying key companies you want to work for** and make speculative applications. If you are lucky, your CV will arrive the week before they go live with a vacancy that is your perfect job.

- **Network with people you know.** Putting pressure on friends makes you a liability and someone to be avoided. Asking people to let you know if they hear of anything that might suit you, gives your friends the chance to help you as and when they can. In my experience people love to help out!

> *'It isn't just what you know, and it isn't just who you know. It's actually who you know, who knows you, and what you do for a living'*
>
> *Bob Burg*

- **Update your profiles on jobsites and LinkedIn.** Make sure that they reflect your new CV and that you have set your search criteria to accept information about new jobs. Also make sure your privacy levels aren't too high and that people can actually make contact with you.

- **Relax, think positive.** You always found a new role in the past and there is every reason to expect you will find one now. If you are currently on the bench, allocate an amount of time every day to your quest (ninety minutes is often perfect) and then make a point of enjoying the rest of your day.

Do some of those jobs you didn't have time to do when you were working. Because very soon you will be...

NOTES

....

....

....

....

....

....

....

....

....

....

....

....

....

....

....

14 – WHAT THE HIRING MANAGER SEES

The holy grail of all documents is the perfect CV. It seems so complicated to get it right and yet it is so imperative that you do. After all, there is absolutely no point sending a CV to someone for it just to go directly to their 'no' pile. It is a waste of your time and effort. Taking the time and paying attention to your creation in the design phase is a much better use of your energy.

Throughout this book, I have talked about perfect CVs and how to create them. But what does a Hiring Manager (or recruiter) see?

Well, let me reiterate the quantity. When I was a recruiter I saw in excess of 300 CVs on the average day. Do you know how long it takes to open 300 emails? Let alone read every one and interpret them by reading between the lines.

The Hiring Manager is looking to make their first shortlist quickly. Your CV will be speed read (the average time each CV gets is four and a half minutes – obvious no's get a lot less!). Make sure your relevant experience is on the front page. Putting a whole tranche of educational information and qualifications first is a mistake. It is like talking about the boot capacity and the tyres on the cover of a car brochure.

Your front page needs to be a summary of your relevant skills and experience followed by your professional / job history; current job first, working backwards. Someone should only ever see the part-time paper round you had whilst you were in sixth-form if they get that far and want to know you better

Often your CV will be sifted for the relevant pile by an administrative assistant or someone from HR who will not know the ins and outs of your job and won't be able to read between the lines. Also, bear in mind that job titles mean different things to different organisations. It is important to explain what you do in full and remember to list your achievements.

A list of anything translates into blah blah blah. If I say to you typing, WordPress and articles what does that mean to you? That's right; nothing! It doesn't say what I do with them, how competent I am or if I am indeed competent at all. If I say to you; 'I type at 60wpm, I am proficient at WordPress; I can manage it from day-to-day, change themes and adapt widgets and plug-ins. I write articles of approximately 700 words which mostly earn me expert author status on Ezine Articles (I've attached three for your consideration)'. That gives you quite an overview of what I can and do do. Do you see how you can make that kind of difference in your CV?

Try to ensure all of your information is self-explanatory, even if that means leaving out some of the things you currently detail and include additional information on other items. It is better to say more about the things that are relevant and make it a document that speaks for itself, than to be vague about a hundred things in an effort to demonstrate that you can do a multitude of tasks and have diverse experience. When a hiring manager is looking for XYZ they want to know what you can do with XYZ, not necessarily that you can recite the entire alphabet.

Become an expert in your field, rather than a Jack (or Jill) of all trades. It won't get you noticed, it will get you deselected.

'How you do anything is how you do everything'

Derek Sivers

A half-hearted, haphazard, disjointed CV indicates that as being your working style. Is that the message you are trying to convey?

Your CV is your own personal marketing brochure; make it great, make it count, make it portray you as the person to call for interview!

NOTES

....

....

....

....

....

....

....

....

....

....

....

....

....

....

....

15 – MATCH.CV

I have been challenged on my belief that CVs should be tailored to match job specifications. There is a view that candidates should proudly display their originally listed experience, so that a potential employer can see the applicant for what they are, because it is more honest. I thought it was such an interesting point that I would include it here within this book

When you read your CV does it sound like you?
My guess is that your CV reflects some elements of your experience and not others. Remember you have four and a half minutes or less to grab the readers attention. You are better to reflect the elements that matter to the potential employer, rather than a set of standard skills which are of little relevance to the role you are applying for

Would you buy a car if all the brochure talked about was the wheels and the size of the boot? (that's a trunk if you're American)
One could argue that you know all cars have engines, all cars have safety features and all cars have 0-60 speeds, so you should take those things as a given and pay attention to the

lesser known facts about the car and let them sway your buying decision. Have I convinced you? No? Now you see why the Hiring Manager isn't convinced either, when he has to imagine all that is not there to tempt and persuade him

Would you be flattered if someone sent you a magazine about deep-sea fishing because they know you like beach holidays; based on the idea that the beach borders the sea, the sea is full of fish ...
Most of us have such a huge overload of data in this age of information that we struggle to keep up and retain interest in the things that genuinely do interest us. When someone sends us a document that is not instantly apparent in its relevance, it is almost a relief that you can just delete it and move on. Wonder where your non-tailored, jack-of-all-trades showing you can turn your hand to anything CV went?

Be an expert. Be proud to know a lot and have achieved many great things in your particular niche. Really focus on XYZ if that is what the job requires.

Make the employers job easy; show them all your relevance to their role. Make it obvious to understand how and why you would be good for this job. They will really thank you for making at least one email a little easier to understand and more exciting for them to open

NOTES

....

....

....

....

....

....

....

....

....

....

....

....

....

....

....

16 – WHAT MORE CAN I DO?

If you love what I have shared with you but are still struggling to get your CV just right and would like us to help then we can do that. Ask me to review what you have prepared, or send me everything in raw format and ask us to create your CV for you; I want you to get the job and I want to work with you to achieve that

We also run webinars where you can talk through your situation and ask your own questions. Everyone that attends live gets their questions answered. Guaranteed!

Whichever way we work together, I will give you my expert opinion and feedback. I have successfully sent out thousands of CVs; I don't have a tracker but we could easily be talking in excess of 10,000. My suggestions and tips come from years of experience working with many thousands of candidates on thousands of vacancies and getting ongoing feedback from hundreds of clients.

If you have been struggling this far, give something different a try, you never know what results you may get.

*'Insanity: doing the same thing over
and over again and expecting
different results'*

Albert Einstein

Email me at churchillbrook@gmail.com to set up a time to chat and I'll see if I can help!

17 – QUICK START GUIDE

1. Decide on the specific type of role you are looking for. Narrow it down. You want to demonstrate that you are experienced and competent in one thing, not a Jack or Jill of all trades and master of none

2. Email us at churchillbrook@gmail.com for a printable PDF of this Quick Start Guide. Also print the job spec of the role you are applying for and the Company bio OR three to four job specs of your dream role as advertised by different organisations

3. On a blank sheet, put your contact details in the header. Your name, along with the month and year in the footer. Now put your name in bold type at the top of the page

4. To start, create a 'Professional Profile' heading. We will come back to this at the end

5. Create a 'Professional Experience' heading. Start with your most recent role. Insert Company name, dates employed and your job title in bold. Then a brief

overview of your role and responsibilities, making sure to note the things asked for in the job spec

6.   Create a list of eight to twelve bullet points, starting with the requirements from all four job specs and reducing down to the ones that are in three, then two. Finishing with your strongest points of things that you have achieved that might not be listed anywhere. These should be completed in achievement style and should answer the job spec requirements, not mirror them. ie sales experience should be answered with 'I have sold X products and services to Y people achieving £Z within the last XYZ period; which put me XY% over target' NOT 'I have five years sales experience' Remember the mantra of the Hiring Manager – what can this person do for me

7.   List the role before, using the same format and listing five to eight bullet points (you can change the focus to this role and make it the more meaty section if your experience was more relevant than that of your current position)

8.   Repeat the above step for the role prior again

9.   List all previous employment, but if you are going back ten years+ then the company name, dates, job title and a brief overview per role is now sufficient. When going back twenty years+ then you can even drop the overview and just list the company name, dates and job title

10. Create a 'Professional Qualifications' heading and list everything you have studied, most relevant first

11. If you have Professional Memberships, have written White Papers, Books, or done anything else remarkable list it next under its own heading

12. Create an 'Education' heading and list your highest academic qualifications. If you have more than one degree then list them all including the subject(s) and the pass grade. If it is A Levels, O Levels or GCSEs it is sufficient to say X (number) (name exam type) including (list best graded or most relevant two or three subjects)

13. If there is anything else that supports your application and is a must-know about you then create an 'Additional Information' heading here

14. We are on to 'Personal Details'. Location, write next to that if you are willing to relocate, work away, be constantly on the road or anything else significant relating to your operational base. Then marital status and possibly driving licence information (ie that you have one) if the role is going be field based

15. Finally 'References'. It is sufficient to say 'references are available on request' without listing names or contact details at this stage

16. NOW, most important, go back to the top and complete your 'Professional Profile'. This should be a couple of short paragraphs, picking out major points that ARE listed within your CV and that reflect the overall requirements of the job spec(s). Make sure that this section matches the rest of your CV. You can start by saying 'I have twenty years experience in ………. ' or whatever is true for you.

17. Spell check, proof read, grammar check and tidy-up the layout. This document creates the employers first impression of you and is your only opportunity to request an interview. Make sure it is good!

NOTES

....

....

....

....

....

....

....

....

....

....

....

....

....

....

....

NOTES

....

....

....

....

....

....

....

....

....

....

....

....

....

....

....

ABOUT THE AUTHOR

Dubbed the Queen of LinkedIn by her friends, and something of a social media darling, Julie Holmwood is the Jobseeker's Guide for Churchill Brook. She works with clients who are frustrated by jobsearch and teaches them how to get that job, using online and offline skills and techniques. She is available to work with limited clients on a one-to-one basis *or* via one of our many audio, video or webinar programmes *or* by joining our weekly teleclass.

Before joining Churchill Brook, Julie spent almost twelve years as an international headhunter, where she successfully helped her clients to recruit exceptional people. Julie is an expert at getting candidates noticed by companies and had one of the highest success ratios for CV submission to hire that we know of within the recruitment industry.

Please go and chat to Julie via her social media connections. You can find her @;

Our Website

On LinkedIn

On Facebook

On Twitter

On YouTube

On Churchill Brook's
Facebook Page

Julie also runs a LinkedIn group entitled <u>The Jobseeker's Guide</u>

She is very social and would love for you to look her up!

ANOTHER BOOK BY THIS AUTHOR

Clickst@rt Your Career

JULIE HOLMWOOD

CONTENTS

1 - USING SOCIAL MEDIA FOR YOUR CAREER

Social media is a hot topic. Facebook is the second most used website in the world (second only to Google) and has more than 845 million active users, over 50% of whom log-in on any given day. Twitter ranks 9th, LinkedIn 12th and WordPress is at number 18. To put this in perspective, Apple, with the best selling iPad and iPhone is at 36 and the BBC is currently at 49.

It seems that our key desire when using the net is to connect with our friends through one medium or another. If you agree with me and the general consensus that word of mouth is the best form of recommendation, it stands to reason that letting your online friends know about your professional status and plans could just net you the opportunities your dreams are made of.

Welcome to the word of mouse! Or should that be the world of mouth!?

Before we go further, I want to point out, if your professional plans include jumping ship from your present employer, your online campaign needs to be tethered with the fact that you, or one of your friends, are linked to your current colleagues and/or boss.

The good and the bad news about social media is that it makes a small world ever smaller. If you are gainfully employed and your Company knows nothing about your desire to spread your wings and fly to pastures new, your advance via social media needs to be covert.

My personal favourite site for career advancement is LinkedIn. A professional site that suggests you post your CV as your profile, it is ideally geared to getting you ahead. You can see people to three degrees and can make contact with your 2nd and 3rd degree network via referral or by upgrading to a business, business plus or pro account which buys you InMail credits.

Headhunters, recruiters and employers themselves love this site and use it regularly to search for candidates to fill current vacancies. If your profile contains keywords that a typical search would include, be assured you are going to be appearing in some shortlists and will no doubt be getting a call or an email to assess your interest in position XYZ.

LinkedIn is also used to search for professional resources: suppliers; people to manage a project with; someone to contribute expertise or an article and public speakers for live events, webinars and tele-seminars.

So, what can you do to help yourself? Well, just as you would shine your shoes and wear a clean suit to a meeting or interview you can clean-up and polish your online profile too;

- Create what you want to post in a package such as Microsoft Word that highlights spelling errors, so that you can make sure there aren't any in your work

- Get a friend to read through what you have written to ensure it is easy to read and makes sense; the best type of friend to do this is one that is not in your industry. A future line manager might understand jargon but a recruiter, HR manager or person looking to create a joint venture won't, so plain English is your best language

- Double check dates as these might be used to cross-reference later

- Write enough to explain what you do, how you do it, who you do it for and why people pick you. To back this up you can ask some select people to write recommendations for you

- Put yourself in your profile visitor's shoes;

  - Does your profile say enough about what you have done and are doing to make them want to know more?

- Do you come across as an honest and open person?

- Do you appear professional and likeable?

Just as someone can tell if you are smiling on a phone-call, so a reader can get this information from a profile.

- Double check your other profiles. Is your message consistent on them all? If your LinkedIn profile is all about customer service and keeping calm under pressure and you are swearing like a trooper over something that was said on the TV via your Facebook page, you are not going to be displaying a calm-under-pressure image.

If you think it is not important, or the sites are not connected, then I will tell you a secret; I joined Facebook on a request from a client who wanted me to verify the character of a candidate.

EXERCISES

- Research where people in your (desired) industry congregate online; is there one site or group within a site that is full of all the movers and the shakers?

- Check your online profiles and see how you are using your online presence. Is it for friendship or business? Are you putting your best foot forward? One way to do a quick check is to ask yourself this question: If the CEO of your dream company were to stumble across you online would they be sending an urgent email to their HR department insisting that they get you on board?

- Look-up a couple of people that currently hold the job you want. What are they saying about themselves? How are they portraying their skills and experience? Where are they and which groups do they belong to?

Decide which elements to use in your own online profiles.

NOTES

....

....

....

....

....

....

....

....

....

....

....

....

....

2 – WHICH SOCIAL MEDIA IS GOING TO HELP YOU

When faced with a busy diary and an active social calendar, spending more time online might not be top of your agenda. But, if you are looking to either change direction, or further your career in some way, then half an hour per day might be just the career workout you are looking for.

There are lots of social media sites. I get invited to a new one I've never heard of, at least once a month. To be found, you need to be where people look. Sticking with the bigger brands is the fastest and easiest way to make that happen. They are already being picked up by the search engines and they are exactly where someone looking for a person just like you (in fact it could even be you) is going to go.

 You can create a personal profile and give a brief career bio in the work and education section of the info tab.

Companies like finding people on Facebook as it gives them an insight into 'you the person' rather than just your professional profile on your CV and in industry news publications.

There are lots of professional pages and groups on Facebook. Like or join the ones that are relevant to your career plans and start making new friends.

Remember, above what you know in terms of importance, is WHO you know. Particularly if they know what you do too!

twitter

If you can put your point over in 140 characters or less this might just be for you. In seriousness it is somewhere to promote your blog, speaking schedule or papers and books you have written / been part of.

It is also somewhere to know and get known by people in your new field if you are looking to change direction. Start by following the people who you admire and then get involved in chat.

A fabulous place to post your CV without saying 'I am posting my CV'.

Link to people in your industry; I used to invite people I met at trade shows to connect. You can also find people in a direction you want to head and start networking for your future.

Chat within the groups. There are some great options, in probably every industry. There are question and answer sessions on XYZ (their topic). Join in. Either: answer some questions; post a thought; or ask something yourself.

Once your name comes up here and there, people will start clicking through to look at your profile and see who you are. If your plan is to make a current hobby into your career, find a way to say that in the summary section.

If you are a public speaker, or you want to develop your career in this direction, then YouTube just might be your new best-friend. Nothing says 'I can', better than 'watch me'.

Get someone to film you speaking at an event, or put together a five minute talk on something of interest in the sector you want to be known for and put it on your YouTube page.

Two ways of being seen are to make some relevant friends on YouTube and to distribute your video via your other social media accounts.

WORDPRESS

If you have a specific skill-set, a vast amount of knowledge on your specialist subject or you are looking to change career direction consider writing a blog.

Experts advise that you blog on a regular basis so that your followers know when to look for you. Regular can, of course, be the first Monday of the month and shouldn't be confused with frequent.

Blogging is a great way to show people that you know your subject and it will gain you a following. This is fantastic news for career enhancement.

If you are looking to change direction and you know a huge amount about your new career path, but lack the job history on your CV, sharing what you know via blogs will get you known within your new field of interest and considered for potential roles.

EXERCISES

- Decide which channels you are going to use to best showcase your skills and experience

- Think about how you want to be known within your chosen field: do you want to be the consummate professional; the sharp wit; the knowledgeable one; the go-to person; super helpful; the upbeat positive influence; the dealmaker; the organiser. How you are and how you want to be known need to lead all of your content!

- Assess where the gaps are between what you want to create and what you already have 'out there'

Notes

....

....

....

....

....

NOTES

....

....

....

....

....

....

....

....

....

....

....

....

....

....

3 – PUBLIC DOMAIN ETIQUETTE

Whenever you post anything on the Internet, run my two double checks; is it ok for your grandmother and is it ok for your best client / boss? If the answer is yes, then post, if the answer is no, go back to your drawing board.

No matter what you think your privacy settings give you and how few people can see your profile, once you post online it is just that, online. Most of the time no-one finds what you post. There are so many people online and so many items being posted every single minute of the day that it would be impossible for everything said by everyone to be read by anyone other than the intended few.

However, once you start going for a new job, pitching for a new client or just generally stepping outside your traditional crowd then it is possible and even likely that someone will want to background check you.

One of the aspects of this kind of search is to run a media check, which looks for times you have appeared in print. You would be amazed what comes up from the deepest darkest archives and you would be even more amazed at how quickly and easily these things are found. One of the many wonders of the modern world and everyone using technology!

There are two very sensible options open to you. Sorry, that should be two options, one infinitely sensible and one that is very limiting. The limiting option is to avoid being online. I have a friend that takes that line. But with 845 million+ people using Facebook, 100 million active Twitter users sending 175 million tweets a day, 150 million using LinkedIn with growth set at one new user per second, over 4 billion videos being watched on YouTube every single day and 70 million blogs on WordPress that is a big market to hide your light from. Particularly if you want your light to be found!

Now some of these people might have an account on all four, so the total number might be nearer 900 million regular social media users, rather than 2.8 billion (which is the total number of online profiles, across these and other channels), but that still narrows your world considerably if you are not there amongst them.

The infinitely sensible option is to only post after running the two checks. This ensures that no matter how high your star rises and what position you go for in the future, what can and might be found about you is going to be ok.

Note: 53% of employers research potential job candidates on social networks. That is not find them, to headhunt. Rather research them, once they already have them in the frame for a role within their company. Over a third found lies in the CV as a result of what was posted by the candidate on a social site. 13% were concerned about discriminatory comments the candidate had made and 9% were offended by provocative or inappropriate photographs. Have you had a great interview, been convinced you were going to get a job offer and then had the opportunity just vanish into thin air? Could your social media presence be the reason?

A consideration I would recommend, for life and your online interaction, is to find nice things to say about people or keep quiet. If everyone is doing the best they can, with what they have, from where they are, giving them the courtesy to be on a learning curve will be appreciated. With that in mind, look for the very best in your friends (old and new) and comment from that place.

As grandmothers around the world are famous for saying; 'manners don't cost anything.' Keep your Ps and Qs in the right order and watch your popularity soar!

EXERCISES

- Check your online profiles including your photo albums AND the photos others have tagged you in. Are they business ready?

- Read through your comments and status updates. Have you been rude, unkind, unfair or just generally grumpy about someone or something? Delete everything that is inappropriate for work eyes; particularly those eyes that don't know you very well yet.

- Run a language check; are there a lot of words you shouldn't use in front of the very young or very old? Effing and jeffing might be the done thing within your group of friends, but unless you work in an industry that promotes swear words, delete the blue comments.

Notes

....

....

....

....

NOTES

....

....

....

....

....

....

....

....

....

....

....

....

....

We hope you enjoyed a taster of Clickst@rt Your Career. The perfect companion for Get That Interview.

To order the book, or download it to your Kindle, please visit Amazon.

3959847R00070

Printed in Great Britain
by Amazon.co.uk, Ltd.,
Marston Gate.